Little Science Stars

Solar System

The Best Start in Science

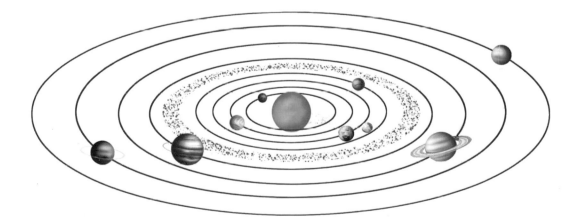

By Helen Orme

ticktock

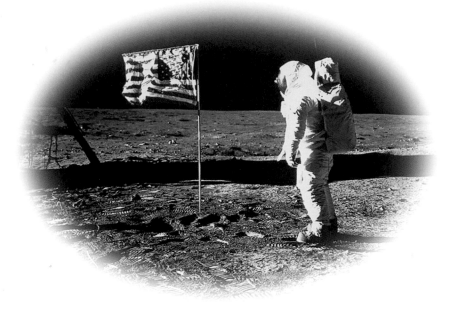

Studio Manager: Sara Greasley
Editor: Rob Cave
Designer: Trudi Webb
Production Controller: Ed Green
Production Manager: Suzy Kelly

ISBN-13: 978 1 84898 053 2 pbk
This revised edition published in 2009 by *ticktock* Media Ltd.

Printed in China
9 8 7 6 5 4 3 2 1

Picture credits (t=top, b=bottom, c=centre, l=left, r=right,
OFC=outside front cover, OBC=outside back cover):
Alamy: 4tr, 9b, 12t, 24br. iStock: OFCt, OFCcl. Meteorite Recon/Wikimedia Commons: 14c, 23c.
NASA: OFCb, 2, 3tl, 3tr, 4tl, 4tc, 5tl, 5tr, 6c, 8tl, 9tl, 12r, 13t, 13br, 14tl, 14bl, 14br, 15tl, 15cl, 16br, 17tl, 17cl, 19b, 20tc, 21t, 21c, 22t, 24t, 24bl, OBC. NASA/JPL: 3tc, 18t, 18c, 19t. Shutterstock: 9c, 12cl, 13c, 14-15 (background), 15r, 16tl, 17tr, 17br, 18b, 20 (main), 20br, 21b.

Every effort has been made to trace the copyright holders and we apologize in advance for any unintentional omissions. We would be pleased to insert the appropriate acknowledgments in any subsequent edition of this publication.

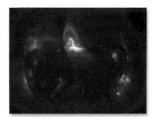  

Contents

Any words appearing in the text in bold, **like this**,
are explained in the Glossary.

What can you see

when you look

at the night sky?

A Galaxy

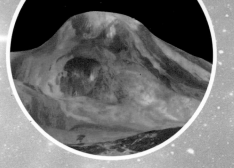

Venus

The Solar System

You might see the Moon.
You might see little bright lights called **stars** or even a **planet**.

The Moon, the planets and a star called the Sun
make up the **Solar System**.

How many planets are there in the Solar System?
What do the planets look like?
Which planet in the Solar System do you live on?

Why is the Sun so important?

The Sun is a small star.

A star makes heat and light.

Without the Sun our planet would always be dark and cold.

The Sun gives the warmth that makes living things grow.

You must NEVER look directly at the Sun. It can blind you.

The Sun is a long way from us, but its heat is so powerful it can burn you if you stay out too long.

The Sun is at the centre of the Solar System. All the other planets travel round (or **orbit**) it.

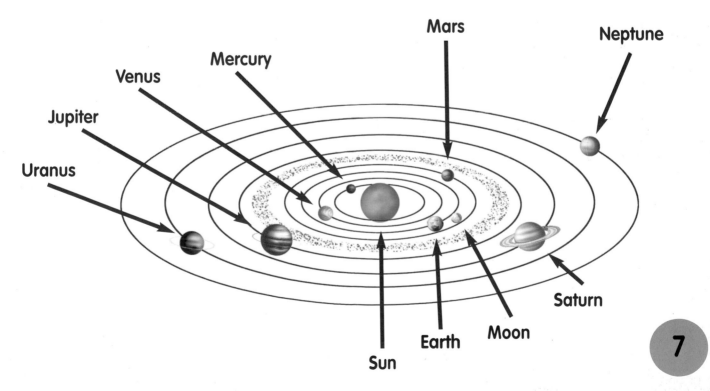

Mars

Neptune

Mercury

Venus

Jupiter

Uranus

Saturn

Moon

Earth

Sun

Which planets are nearest to the Sun?

Mercury

Venus

Mercury is the nearest planet to the Sun.

Mercury is the smallest of all the planets.

Venus is the second planet from the Sun. It is very, very hot.

The Sun

Mars

Saturn

Venus

Earth

Mercury

Jupiter

Uranus

8

Venus is also covered with **acid** clouds and an **atmosphere** so dangerous nothing can live there.

Using a **telescope** you can see Venus rising before the Sun comes up.

Neptune

Which planet is a good place to live?

The Earth is our home. The Earth is a good place to live. It is neither too hot nor too cold.

It is the only planet that we know of where people, animals and plants can live.

A lot of the **surface** is covered with water. All living things need water to drink.

The Earth's air also has enough **oxygen** to let us breathe.

The Earth is just right for all types of life.

From the very tiny...
...to the very large!

Why does the Moon change shape?

The Moon is always circling the Earth.

Half of the Moon is lit by the Sun and half is in **shadow**. Different amounts of the Moon's face are lit up depending on where the Moon is. This is why the Moon appears to change shape.

We know a lot about the Moon because it has been visited by **space probes** and by **astronauts** in **space**.

The Moon has no water, no weather and no air.

The surface of the Moon is covered with holes called **craters**. They were made when lumps of rock from space hit the Moon.

When astronauts visited the Moon they had to wear special **spacesuits** to help them breathe.

Why is Mars called the Red Planet?

When you see Mars through a telescope it looks quite red.

This is because it has very red soil.

Mars is smaller than Earth. It has the biggest **volcano** in the Solar System.

A volcano on Mars

No astronaut has ever gone to Mars, but space probes have visited it.

It takes about six months to reach Mars.

Scientists know there is frozen water on Mars.

They also think they have found **fossil bacteria** on rocks from Mars. This makes some people think there was once life there.

Which planets are the biggest?

The Solar System has two giant planets.

Jupiter

Saturn

They are Jupiter and Saturn.

Saturn has rings. They are made of rock, dust and ice.

Jupiter is the biggest planet in the Solar System.

It is twice as large as all the other planets put together.

Through a powerful telescope you can see that Jupiter has clouds of colourful **gas**.

Red Spot

Jupiter also has a giant red spot. This is actually a massive storm that has been blowing for years.

Which planets are farthest away from us?

Uranus and Neptune are far, far away from the Sun.

Neptune

Uranus

Because they are so far away from the Sun, they are cold, icy planets, colder than the coldest place on Earth.

These planets are very stormy places. Neptune has a storm spot just like the one on Jupiter.

Pluto is a dwarf planet. It is farther away from the Sun than Neptune. We don't know much about it.

A space probe called New Horizons will visit Pluto in 2015 to find out more.

What is Deep Space?

Deep Space includes everything in the **Universe** beyond the Solar System.

Our Solar System is just a tiny part of a **galaxy** called the **Milky Way**. There are many other galaxies too.

This includes not just the planets, but small pieces of loose rock inside the Solar System. When they fall to Earth, they are called **meteorites**.

Sometimes much bigger rocks called **asteroids** crash into Earth. This huge crater was made by an asteroid.

Scientists use special equipment to look beyond the Solar System.

In 1990 **NASA** launched the Hubble Space Telescope. It can see far out into space.

Scientists even send space probes to photograph stars we cannot see from Earth.

In case they make contact with other **life forms**, some space probes carry discs telling listeners things about us and our planet.

Questions and answers

Q What is the biggest planet in the Solar System?

A Jupiter is the biggest planet in the Solar System.

Q How many people have visited the Moon?

A Only 12 people have visited the Moon.

Q How many rings does Saturn have?

A When the Voyager **spacecraft** flew past Saturn, it counted thousands of rings.

Q How long would it take a person to walk to the Sun?

A It would take a person nearly 3,000 years to walk to the Sun.

Q Which planet is closest to the Sun?

A Mercury is the closest planet to the Sun.

Q What space probe is going to visit Pluto in 2015?

A New Horizons is going to visit Pluto in 2015.

Q Why is Mars called the Red Planet?

A Mars is called the Red Planet because of the colour of its soil.

Q What is Deep Space?

A The area outside the Solar System is called Deep Space.

 # Glossary

Acid A chemical substance that can burn or eat away at things.

Asteroids Large rocks in space the size of small planets.

Astronauts People who travel in space.

Atmosphere The air that surrounds a planet.

Craters Holes in a surface made by rocks hitting it.

Deep Space The area of the Universe beyond Earth.

Fossil bacteria The remains of tiny organisms (living things) that lived in an earlier time and became embedded in rock.

Galaxy A huge grouping of stars.

Gas When some things are heated they turn into a gas.

Life forms Living things.

Milky Way The galaxy where our solar system is located.

Meteorites Chunks of rock that have fallen to Earth.

NASA (National Aeronautics and Space Administration) An organisation in the USA for space exploration.

Orbit To move round something in a set path.

Oxygen A gas that makes up part of the air people and animals breathe.

Planet A ball of rock or gas that goes round (orbits) the Sun.

Shadow Dark area created by the blocking of light.

Solar System The Sun, Earth and planets that go round the Sun.

Spacecraft A ship made to travel in space.

Spacesuits Clothes astronauts wear to protect them in space.

Space probes Spacecraft without people that explore space.

Stars Large balls of burning gas, far away in space.

Surface The outside part of something.

Telescope Something that makes things seem closer.

Volcano A place where melted rocks come to the surface.

Universe Everything in space, including the Solar System and galaxies.

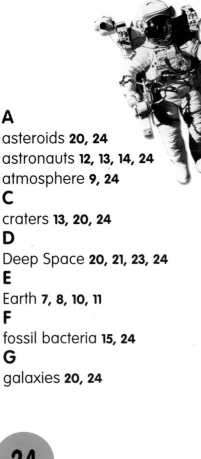

Index